WHAT THE HEART WEIGHS

WHAT THE HEART WEIGHS

Poems

Richard Beban

Red Hen Press ☙ Los Angeles

Cover art
The Judgement of the Dead in the Presence of Osiris
© The Trustees of the British Museum

Book design by Michael Vukadinovich
Cover Design by Mark E. Cull

ISBN 1-888996-48-X
Library of Congress Catalog Card Number 2004096080

Published by Red Hen Press

The City of Los Angeles Cultural Affairs Department,
California Arts Council and
the Los Angeles County Arts Commission
partially support Red Hen Press.

Printed in Canada
First Edition

Acknowledgements

Thanks to teachers: Vivian Beban, Eloise Klein Healy, Chris Abani, Richard Garcia, Adrianne Marcus, Bette Reese, Laurel Ann Bogen, Carolyn Kizer, Alexander & Jane Winslow Eliot, Richard Friedman.

Grateful thanks to David St. John and his master class: Jeanette Clough, Kaaren Kitchell, Beverly Lafontaine, Jim Natal, Jamie O'Halloran, Jan Wesley. To Kimo & to Phil, for the friendship of men, an incalculable commodity. And to Sam & Betty, for everything.

To the gods & goddesses, for daily guidance.

Thanks to the publications in which these poems first appeared, some in variant forms:
The Voyage won a first place in the 2001 *Poetry In the Windows* contest in Highland Park, California, & appears in the chapbook *Richard Beban: Greatest Hits* (Pudding House, 2002); *Genealogy* appeared in Vol. No. (1998); *My Parents Watch the July Fourth Parade* appeared in *On Target* (*Sabado Gigante #2*, 1996), in the chapbook *Fried Eggs With Lace (*Canned Spaghetti Press, 1996*),* in *Richard Beban: Greatest Hits*, & won a first place from the 1997 *Morris Center for Healing* Poetry Contest; *1960: Playing in the Mirrored Hallway of the New Mission Theater While* Psycho *Unreels Within* appeared in the 1999 *Beyond the Valley of the Contemporary Poets* anthology, & in *Richard Beban: Greatest Hits*; *Save the Last Dance for Me* appeared in *Spillway* Issue #8 (1997) & in *Fried Eggs With Lace; My Father & I Shopped* appeared in the anthology *Foreshock* (1995), in *Fried Eggs With Lace,* the online journal *Snakeskin* (1996), in *Richard Beban: Greatest Hits*, & in the anthology *The Art of Pilgrimage* (Conari Press, 1998); *Impression: Boy on the Bridge* appeared in the 1999 *Beyond the Valley of the Contemporary Poets* anthology, & was nominated by the editors for a Pushcart Prize. It also appears in *Richard Beban: Greatest Hits.*
Kite appeared in rivertalk (2002); *My Grandmother Told Us Jokes* appeared in the anthology *What Have You Lost* (Greenwillow, 1999),

Rattle, Issue #9 (1998), in *Fried Eggs With Lace,* & in *Richard Beban: Greatest Hits; Slave to Love: Paris 1986* won an honorable mention in the San Gabriel Valley Poetry Festival & appeared in the SGVPF anthology in 2000; *The Persistence of Vision* appeared in *Quantum Tao* #4 (1999); *Untitled Hopper* appeared in *Cider Press Review,* Issue #1 (2000); *Dancing with the One-Legged Man* appeared in *Perihelion* (2000); *To Bruges, Which Was Once a Seaport* appeared in *Solo,* Issue #5 (2001); *Customer Satisfaction* appeared in *Richard Beban: Greatest Hits; What the Heart Weighs* appeared in the chapbook *I Burn for You* (Inevitable Press, 1999), in *Richard Beban: Greatest Hits* & in *Poeticdiversity* (2004); *Our Lady of the Pigeons* appeared in *Solo,* Issue #3 (1999); *The Ascension* appeared in *Psychological Perspectives* (1999) & in *Richard Beban: Greatest Hits; Silence* appeared in the anthologies *Bedside Prayers* (Harper SanFrancisco, 1997) & *Bless the Day* (Kondasha America, 1998); *Sisyphus' Day Runner* appeared in *rivertalk* (1999); *All the Hits, All the Time* appeared in *Perihelion* (2000); *The Psychiatrist, Narcissus, Writes Up His Findings on Jekyll & Hyde* won a first place in the 1999 *Poetry In the Windows* contest in Highland Park, California; *One of a Chorus of Angels* appeared in *Perihelion* (2000); *Thoughts While Unpacking After Septum Undeviation* appeared in *Blue Satellite* (1999); *The Proctor Will Have Instructions* appeared in Fourth Street (2002); *Birdwatching with Marley* appeared in rivertalk (2001). *Ordinary Birds* appeared in *Urban Spaghetti* (1999); *On Guardian Angels* appeared in the anthology *Heal Your Soul, Heal the World* (Andrews McMeel, 1998), in *Urban Spaghetti* (1999); in *Richard Beban: Greatest Hits,* in the anthology *Animal Blessings* (Harper SanFrancisco, 2000), & in the anthology *Looking for God in All the Right Places* (Loyola Press, 2004); *Talking to Birds* appeared in *Urban Spaghetti* (1999); *The Quail* appeared in *rivertalk* (2001); *The Artist's Way* is a revision of *Matisse in Black & White,* which appeared in *Spillway,* Issue #9 (1999); *Summer Rain Sonnet for the Average Housefly* appeared in the anthology *How Luminous the Wildflowers* (Tebot Bach, 2003); *I Burn for You, She Asks Us Both to Imagine the Relationship Won't Last, In India the Stone Temple Gods,* &

Liebestod all appeared in the chapbook *I Burn for You; In India the Stone Temple Gods* also appeared in the anthology *Knowing Stones* (Burke 2000), & *Liebestod* also appeared in *Richard Beban: Greatest Hits*; *Aubade* appeared in *Solo*, Issue 7 (2004); *Opossum* appeared in the chapbooks *I Burn for You* & *Richard Beban: Greatest Hits*.

Richard Beban can be reached at: beban@beban.org

Contents

What the Heart Weighs

Sisyphus' Day Runner

Talking to Birds

Liebestod

Without Kaaren, none of this would be possible.
Especially the impossible.

THE VOYAGE

Li Po folded his poems into paper boats,
set them out upon the river, uncertain
they, he, or the world would survive.

He knew the river merged with something
grander, but that was itself a beginning,
not a destination at all. By the time the poems

arrived, the ink had leached from the sodden
paper, pictographs became dark eddies,
whirlpools into which meaning was sucked

& drowned. The once-words spread like
shadows over the gathered water, broke into
waves & set out for distant lands.

THE WAY THE GAME WAS PLAYED

Rules Learned From a Bottle of Liquid Detergent[†]

Keep Joy out of the reach of children.
If Joy gets in your eyes,
rinse thoroughly
with water. If swallowed,
drink a glass of water to dilute.

[†]*A found poem, courtesy of an anonymous Procter & Gamble copywriter.*

GENEALOGY

We return to our story, Grandpa's eager hands
sculpt his daughter's clay, push her out of
the house at seventeen, the trembling boy

who cupped her like a gift, too soon
found the price was youth, the children
who followed, most in their parents' footsteps

raised by children, they hammer & sculpt
children & the story goes on, generation
is the easy part after generation is not.

Some children shatter, marble struck
too hard, the chisel found fault & still probed.
Some children crack in the heat of the kiln

perfectly glazed but broken inside. Some stand
in the winter garden, cold & bronze, cast there by
indifference. Some melt like lost wax & run away.

My Parents Watch the July Fourth Parade

Perhaps they were both dyslexic;
never clear on the difference
between marital & martial.

Thought the wedding march was
by John Phillip Sousa or Francis
Scott Key—bombs bursting in

the living room, kitchen, beat of
muffled drums, sharp staccato
racket of sticks on rims, crack of

ribs, crack of small arms fire,
small children abandoned in the
corners like spent shell casings.

The stars & stripes forever
imprinted—stars as blows hit the
skull, stripes from the slashing leather

belt across the backs of thighs. Red
welts, white skin, blue bruises never
shown at school where you stood for the

Pledge of Allegiance & learned how fine
a country this is & why our parents fought
so hard to keep it free. Learned the price

of war was high, but teacher said it
was worth it. Look at all we had
that children in other countries wanted.

FAIL-SAFE

Death will come from the sky.
It will sound like thunder &
fire will fall. It will be a flash
so bright your child eyes will know
wonder the instant before they
melt & flow from their sockets
like an archangel's tears.

But do not fear. Even if all that is left
of you is your shadow scorched
into the asphalt schoolyard, the small
piece of steel at the pulse in your throat,
with your blood type & your home
address, will tell your parents it is you.
They will have a token that says:
This was my child.

Each time a jet screams overhead
you will remember to duck
& cover—or when you wake in a dark
unfamiliar house because the low roar
of water in the pipes has disturbed your dreams.
The gift of Oppenheimer & Einstein
is that first adrenaline pump
until you get your bearings. You will feel for
your eyes, & their fragile roundness
through your lids
will reassure you: *Not yet.*

THE WAY THE GAME WAS PLAYED

Our football was a rolled-up *Chronicle*,
wrapped tight with shiny friction tape.
Long passes spiraled end over end
& came down hard against the arm,
bruised a boy's biceps if caught without
exquisite care. Each lasted only a Sunday
or two, scuffed into feathery shreds from
scrapes against unforgiving pavement.
Then Dad would roll another hard, tight,
overlap the black tape, sealing the words inside
& we would run downfield, dodging among
the parked cars to confuse defenders,
looking back over our shoulders, fingers
tingling, anticipating the long bomb.

1960: PLAYING IN THE MIRRORED HALLWAY OF THE NEW MISSION THEATER WHILE *PSYCHO* UNREELS WITHIN

I am myself but ever
smaller & smaller—
edges fade, darken,
recede into murky
worlds light swallows
like the fearful gods
who ate their
young. Inside the hushed
theater Martin Balsam climbs
those stairs one more time,
crisp, indelible
celluloid sharper than the knife
he will know in seconds,
end his world-weary
shuffle with a tumble back
down Mrs. Bates' carefully carpeted
risers. In the upstairs hallway
between balcony doors
I raise one arm &
the legions of those not me
but like me mimic the motion.
I spin to see the back
of myself, hidden over my shoulder,
but those behind me are
too fleet, reveal only
one face, infinite gest-
ure, thirteen forever, too young
to know how time folds in
on itself like a pocket
knife. I follow the endless
selves inside
the smooth, silent, reflective world.

KITE

I remember the string yanking tight
around Father's ankle,
as Brother carefully played

it out, letting the stick turn against
his palms. Father rose on the wind,
arms outstretched, bobbed side-to-side,

splayed fingers feeling his way up unseen
thermals. I worried about his glasses
falling from such a height, but as he grew

smaller I saw them neatly folded
in their case at Brother's feet.
A gust of raw April billowed his red

windbreaker, pulled Father higher, the corded
muscles of Brother's bare arms cable-thick
as he fought the wind, the whirling stick

gouging holes in his palms, his flesh opaque,
then pink, then bursting into flame
as he let go & Father wafted east

well above the skyscrapers & the
diamond-sparkled bay, whatever he was
calling back lost in the wind.

Save the Last Dance For Me

My brother still plays vinyl.
Weighs down the tone arm
of his record player with
more & more pennies,
stacked on, taped on, so
the needle will never jump
out of the groove.

The old music soothes him, doo-wop,
three-chord rock, slow ballads with strings,
easy dances from an easier time
he won't leave.

It was the best time, he says
of 1961, when he was fifteen
going on sixteen & The Drifters'
"Save the Last Dance For Me"
was barely a year old.

He knows by heart the color
of every 45 record label,
coral, orange, red, yellow, black—
on Capitol, Argo, VeeJay, Tamla, Everlast—
what was on the flip side,
how long the cut,
how high it peaked
on the Billboard chart.

The music plays, drowns the sound
of father's drunken beatings, of mother's
obsessive attention to his erupting
skin, the constant wails of miserable
siblings he, as firstborn, was forced to raise.

With the sound cranked loud he can't hear the
crackle of coral, orange, red, yellow, black
from our childhood house, the one he
set fire to, consuming his own rage
in those dancing flames.

My Father & I Shopped

in the street market
along the rue Mouffetard
amid the babble of accents,
the recent immigrants:
dark faces from Cameroon,
the oranges from North Africa,
brown skins from Algeria,
fragrant, ghost white mushrooms
from the dark earth of Brittany,
the ancient gray Parisians;
herbs & peppers & vegetables—
reds, greens, & yellows, each distinct,
luminous in the overcast.

When we returned to our rented flat
he napped, tired from the short walk.

I sliced two large tomatoes in rounds
drained them, picked basil,
dried the muted green leaves,
sliced the spongy white mozzarella,
remembering the way he sliced salami when I was young,
precise, paper-thin, an astonishing number of slices
from a single, stubby sausage.

On two white porcelain plates I interleaved
tomato, mozzarella, basil.

When I heard him in the bathroom, shaking out
the ration of pills that were buying him the extra days,
I drizzled golden olive oil over the salads,
set them on the table
with red linen napkins,
with polished silver.

Before he ate, he photographed his plate.

Impression: Boy on the Bridge

One: April 1944

Buried in grandmother's scrapbook
a boy of 16 leans, in black & white,
back against the girder of a railroad

bridge—shirt off, proud chest,
skin smooth, high above a river
we cannot see. His dark hair is

full & wavy, half-lidded eyes
bright. The old Kodak caught noon
so sharp, & soft reflection of river light,

but does not reveal the crippled arm
that kept him from war, or his reckless
quest for manhood that ends soon

in a girl of 17. Virgins lie together & get up
parents, & in their fertile act will die
his dreams of art school, hers of handprints

at Grauman's Chinese. He will drink, she
will eat, they will pass their fractures to five
children before their constellation drains of light.

Two: April 1986

A man leans on a small stone bridge just west
of Notre Dame, not a mile from those blue
Monets, the yellow Van Goghs they saw

on the trip he gave his father a year before.
He stares through drizzle into the sluggish
Seine, cradles a small golden box. Which of

these coarse white chips came from the boy's
bare chest, he wonders, which are the crippled
arm? The fine, gray ash could be pigment

painters use in the technique called
grisaille; or it could be the final mix of yellow,
red & blue, when each surrenders its individual

hue. At the stroke of noon the son
upends the box. White chips, gray powder
catch the breeze, smoothly arc, then settle

on the water. What is left of the boy
drifts past the grand cathedral,
joins the soft river light.

MY GRANDMOTHER TOLD US JOKES

like the one about the man who
walked down the street
& turned into
a drugstore.

There was some secret in the moment
of that turning—when he was one thing,
became another—
that I return to again & again.

The day she stopped being
grandma & turned into
that madwoman.

The day my sister stopped being
& never came back. Perhaps there
was an instant between her sweet sleep

& the moment the fever struck,
from which she could have been plucked.

Do not make that turn, I want to say to the man
who becomes the drugstore; to the woman
who dies insane; to my sister;

to the boy who became an adult
the moment the cell door slammed shut.
I want to freeze-frame each instant of turning,

unfold in slow motion the moment of callous
change. Perhaps the secret's in the man's
intention; in the list in his pocket of mundane
nostrums he was sent to fetch home.

Or perhaps I've got it wrong,
perhaps there's a soda fountain where they all sit—
the man, my grandmother, my sister, the boy—

& drink nickel root beer floats, look back
on that fateful turn, & laugh among themselves
at the rest of us, who took it all so seriously.

SLAVE TO LOVE

Lives of the Poets: Chapter One

"[Akhmatova] was slow to accept his proposal. He sought her
attention by repeated attempts at suicide until she finally
married him in 1910."
> —Jane Kenyon, from the introduction to
> *Twenty Poems of Anna Akhmatova.*

The way to a woman's heart is through
the emergency room. Just follow that
thready blue vein there at the pulse.

Or the churning, gurgling stomach
pump, the furrow cut by the miraculous
bullet that somehow only grazed the skull—

roulette played with hearts, & fear for tokens.
Anna, what were you thinking? Stubborn
schoolgirl eventually swayed by theater

of the absurd? *No,* you say, *it was like this:*
Called to the doctor's rooms that final time,
I stepped down from the carriage & saw

by dawn light against the omnipresent white,
the first red crocus of spring.

SLAVE TO LOVE: PARIS 1986

In the *Place Contrescarpe* we conspired
to cut his silk shorts to shreds, your dark
Italian who whispered "everything,"
but meant only that he would take it all.

The snaggle-toothed waiter brought me
creme after *café creme*, for you more
vin rouge in small tumblers. You said
you held it well, but you didn't. Your hands
never shook, but your face wore the full, red
October moon & your tongue grew
a coating of mud.

We tithed francs to the jukebox,
heard *Slave to Love* again & again
& laughed. That was yesterday,
we vowed, the clank of manacles
almost drowning our words. I toasted
the woman I came here to forget, her name
cut my lips like sharp winter breath.

He was proudest of his silk underwear,
you said, how it felt against his scrotal sac
& the head of his tasty *cannoli*. He was hard
most of the time & you took that
for love but never again. One more
vin rouge, one more taste
of Brian Ferry's liquid voice
& you would be off, carving knife
in your purse, key to his apartment
in your palm. But you slid into November
& the francs ran out & Kansas suddenly
seemed like home again.

The next day you flew there & buried
the knife in the backyard with your copy of
Slave to Love. Your new hometown
husband knows nothing, though he wonders
when he sees in certain oblique prairie light
the deep chafe marks
on your wrists & ankles.

DINNER & CONVERSATION, ATHENS

Susie guts two fish,
slips a knife
in the anus,
slices up the belly
to the neck, spills the red guts
onto the wooden cutting board.
She scales them, bodies held
underwater in a bowl by the sink,
all the time talking of ex-lovers,
who would not leave their wives
for her.

By the time we eat
the fishes' eyes have gone gray,
steamed into cataracts,
& the old lovers
are picked clean
as the fine bones.

The Persistence of Vision

What impresses the eye is never apparent
at first glance. But shut them
& see what lingers there. Seared
on the retina. White
becomes black. Complementary colors
reveal more than was first seen.

Science calls this the persistence
of vision. How you linger,
year after year
on my closed eyes, in the
unprotected space in my heart;
the whites of your eyes gone dark,
promises flickering like hallucinations
at the edge.

REUNION

The thread of silence knit
guest, host
white chrysanthemum.
          —*Ryota (1718-1787)*[†]

The flower is not all that blossoms
between us. There is the time we spent,
so short, & the time since, so long. I wrote

the script for dinner, apologies
refined—yours & mine—to haiku. How few
syllables it would take to make the past

bloom again, the interval seem a mere
blink. But look closely: See how different
each petal is. "White" is yellow here, alabaster

there, ivory & cream, snow; even the
speckled marble of a sepulcher.
If light is so inconstant, petal to

petal, what then can we now say of love?

[†]Translation by author from Henderson

Untitled Hopper

Is it sex, or war
when cats convene
under the house,
keening moans & wails,
almost words
in the guttural
mumbles. Who knows those
subtle signs of demarcation,
the word for
territory in an
indecipherable language?

Imagine them
in a Hopper canvas—
how far apart would they sit,
how much counter space between
them for comfort? Imagine
the muted yellow distance
between walls of a cheap suite,
once pastel, now grimy
with cigarette smoke
& diesel soot. Imagine staring

out of that window to a landscape beyond
the frame, tin promises in your eyes,
your partner, distant in the
living room's stuffed chair, newspaper
blocking the face
behind the neat columns
of ink & rotogravure.

Imagine the yowl
from your own throat confined
by the hard wooden edges.

DANCING WITH THE ONE-LEGGED MAN

When the one-legged man suddenly grew
his leg back, everything changed
& nothing. He danced new steps
but with the same herky-jerky, one-pistoned
gait. We all sang hosannas for him,
clapped a new rhythm
to his step, prayed for
lightness. Not that this actually happened,

but when my friend Jake—
after thirty years of whining
obesity, throwing up in the sink
to top off capacious meals, incapacitated
by the slightest hint of the mating dance—
found Sally & she married him,
we all hopped the night away like the
one-legged man in that legendary
ass-kicking festival. Not that this lasted—

the night, the dance, or the music. Inside
this whining fat man was
a whining fat man trying
to get out. The brief spark
snuffed when Sally left, tired
of the piston's monotonous
grind & chuff. That's
Jake we see alone again
dancing, herky-jerky, still humming
the only tune he knows.

To Bruges, Which Was Once a Seaport

for James Wright

How you felt your beloved sea's desertion—
mourning its tender caress at stone flanks,
moan of wet rope & curved timber, whipcrack
of breeze-blown colored pennants, tall masts,
sails full & round like the mountains you could
only imagine from this low place. How
bitter salt caked when last tide receded,
silt rose & choked the harbor, slow drowning
in mute sand, dreams damned in levees & dikes.
The babble of tongues has died—rough patois
of slaves, spicy slang of sailors—cargoes
carried from places whose names are now lost
to wind that only rustles lace curtains,
gauze bandaging a husk that does not heal.

deTocqueville's Truck Stop

DeTocqueville's Truck Stop

the god of truckstops
makes his wishes known
in neon

his commandments blink
from a distance:

Eat   he says
Gas   Diesel   & Beer

his people are doughy
lank   most in need

of ministration
or dentists   to excavate
below the film
of vended peanut butter
crackers & thin cherry slushes

kindness has gone
south   or just over the ridge
or someone read about it in the next town
& has a faded clipping
corners held in yellowed tape
by the register flanking the beer nuts

small things made of wood
on the counter   lift the indian's thin pine breechcloth
see his memory rise & point
toward the shelf of carved & vanished buffalo

the world's chenille bedspreads are kept
inside the dusky rooms just beyond
the gas pumps   tiny pink pom-poms yield
to the faces of truckers
each shroud   the proprietor swears
is a relic of the true crossing
the stained sheets speak
of minor saints
whose names might be etched
in the gilt-edged book
in the bedside stand

someone moans
on the radio behind the wall as thin
as its cracked case

dust devils
line the road   thumbs out

there is a town   the descendants of Coronado &
the conquered swear
just over the rise   gold
sunsets   silver rails lead there

MIAMI, JULY, MIDNIGHT

Young girls float in the hotel pool
until they pucker, tread water;
long hair spread like palm fans,
their thin voices rise like heat,
Spanish phrases giggle past tenth
floor window into midnight
blue skies. In Biscayne Bay, pale lights
of ships idle on the water,
near a subtly arching causeway, its strand
of yellow bulbs like rosary beads
through the fingers of *duenas*. Behind
the window of the Washington Street
botanica, perfumes with names like
Taming the Bull; Cast off Evil;
Balsama Tranquillo; Spellbreaker;
Yo Puedo Mas Que Tu[†];
Destroy Everything.

[†]*I overpower you*

SALISHAN BEACH: DEAD OF WINTER

Sleek, svelte, maybe four hundred pounds gross weight,
this teardrop-shaped seal lying parallel
to obsidian, white-crested waves creates

a hillock on the winter shore. Expelled
by the chilly sea, she's been left to rest
at the scrimshawed high-water mark, propelled,

then beached by the deserting tide. Blessed
with soft, flawless fur marbled black & gray,
like ink-swirled paper etched with the finest

calligraphy—she's as lovely today
as Circe or the mermaids myth-spawned from
sailors' wine-dark dreams. In death, she displays

more grace than I can exhibit in dumb-
struck life. *Why* this *sweet young beast*? I wonder,
then remember one death's nothing here. Some

perfectly natural cause has sundered
her life thread. At the edge, only profuse
death prompts official inquiry. Under-

takers gather—six black-beaked gulls who roost
casually on a log. They've begun
by excising her eye. Clearly they're used

to this: not at all shaken or undone
by delicate lashes framing oblivion.

How Little Will Satisfy

How little will satisfy a fruit fly.

I dropped an inside banana rind
thread, whatever those are called.
Sure enough, a fruit fly found it
& gorged happily. I left it where it lay,
a magnanimous act.

How little will satisfy a house pet.

I have a mongrel cat, lives on leftovers,
spaghetti, chicken salad. I'll ask him
what he wants, deferentially he'll say,
*What you're having is fine. Oh, & a bowl
of clean water.* Since Americans shell out
nine billion a year on pet food,
he's not just well mannered;
he's like money in the bank.

How little will satisfy a Chinese

farmer, an Igbo, a Pakistani, a Kurd—the
world's 1½ billion who find their water
in brown puddles, brackish wells,
stagnant ponds & rivers that do double-duty.
As I towel dry from my morning shower
my cat loves to lick my ankles,
my feet, to get the cool drops
of clean water I missed.

In Praise of Los Angeles

Here, in a land "without seasons," we don't
wait for weather to tell us what to do.
From the east we absorb hordes of surprised
refugees—topcoats, greatcoats, winter
armor obsolete here. They are not used
to subtlety, trees that refuse to shed.
Spring is a nuance in the air; purple
jacaranda surprise late April
into turning May. Our April is not
preceded by thick, white clouds of breath
& wool. It is simply ascension from March,
a warmer February, cessation
'til October of January rain.
Here, December white is bleached southern sun,
sand along Venice boardwalk, whitewashed
stucco mimicking Mykonos.

Those married to seasons are queasy;
angry at the absence of "real change" they
pine for the mixed colors of maples,
as if Santa Ana-fueled fires
& the occasional earthquakes are not
change enough. They live lives unsettled by
a lack of overt cues, & miss the baby
sparrows, monarchs & cabbage moths, miss
the mixed colors their children are turning.

CUSTOMER SATISFACTION

In memory of Lucky Supermarkets,
now become Albertson's

At Lucky one noon I found
the smoothest-riding
grocery cart I've ever been dealt,
plucked from the long, hangdog line
of rusted chrome servants
that queue by the door.
The carts are like small cages
in which we temporarily store our wants,
as if our wants can be contained
for any time at all—or sated
by what the supermarket holds. We call it Lucky,
in the hope that they can be.

This cart, at my slightest touch,
broke easily from the herd,
a good omen. Sometimes a recalcitrant cart
will choose to thwart your desire
by tangling with a mate
or two, or three,
a talent learned from
wire coat hangers.
Perhaps metal has genetic memories
of how to perform that trick—that's why
it lasts so long, unlike delicate
human flesh.

This cart pulled free with such grace
that my gentlest tug sailed it
into a light pirouette. I spun to catch this rubber-wheeled
Dame Margot, surprised my stocky form
could move like Nureyev. I was suddenly reborn—
a master shopper finally matched
with the partner
I had long desired.

How we pas-de-deuxed
through the crowded aisles,
neatly dodging a display of Keebler's cookies
constricting that essential artery—
breads & cookies, aisle three.
We zigged & we zagged
down aisles four, five & six—
gliding past gimcracks & geegaws laid to block
our path & pump up our impulses.

We made an impeccable U-turn in aisle eight—
Oh God, what a turning radius! —
around the elderly ladies who cluster
in front of paper products comparing coupons
& the deaths of friends.

And all the way I loaded this cart
with my own obsessions—
the childish satisfaction of morning oatmeal,
the sticky pleasure of peanut butter,
the guilty rush of jam. For my health,
fat-free turkey, easy to slice & gobble
on the run. For show, the veggies
that rot in the fridge
in their out-of-sight compartment
because I am too lazy to make the salads
I know are best for me. I could tell this cart anything,
without embarrassment.
Load all of my weaknesses into it
& have them carried, without a bump,
a catch, or a splayed-out shimmy wheel.
It didn't pull to either side; it pranced straight
like a model on a runway, with purpose,
a beautiful thing.

I don't remember how many hours I spent
in that fluorescent fantasia,
wheeling the aisles, filling the cart.
I suppose the credit card bill
will also bring regret. All I remember next is
the parking lot, the soft light of sunset,
that fleeting instant of golden dusk
filmmakers call "magic hour." I unloaded
the final, crinkly, plastic sack, closed the van's
bulging back end, & we stood together, the empty cart
& I. I thought for a moment of twisting
yarn around the handle,
so I could pick it out again,
but I could sense the truth,
this was all there was between us,
this cart wanted its freedom—
the right, the obligation, to serve others,
like a courtesan, born to please, never to settle.

I reached out a trembling finger to say goodbye,
to stroke one last time its wide, plastic grip,
& that force alone propelled it back,
past the rumps of Jeeps & Range Rovers,
past the fins of Fifties classics,
down that wide, white-striped parking lot
toward the never-closed doors
of that 24-hour casino of commerce—
that place where once I was Lucky,
& set it free.

WHAT THE HEART WEIGHS

WHAT THE HEART WEIGHS

In the Catacombs, Paris 1997

Death is bones the color of leather,
death is a skull with sockets like lace.

We spiral down & down like a feather
caught in a column of air; we face
the walls that twist & tighten & stone
steps that refuse to echo our feet. We turn
& turn & dizzy we finally halt,
thirty meters below the Paris sun.

The air still & cold, Lord, so cold,
the gush of blood in each ear silenced.

We thread long narrow lanes to
visit the dead by the thousands,
freed of the weight of viscera, of love,
their long bones hollow save for
capillaries stilled to petrified foam.

My body hangs heavy from my shoulders,
a cape I wear of organs & flesh. My face
the flat stare of Renoir's woman
stunned on absinthe.

———

The Egyptians claimed at the moment of death
the heart was weighed in the underworld
by the goddess Ma'at against a feather of truth—
light hearts gained the afterlife,
the heavy were devoured by a demon.

I think how much like gods our parents—
wounded gods inventing gods as clues
to their own fallibility. Cruel mother
once-removed
to stepmother or witch
so children can bear her split
as both source of life
& slayer.

———•———

& as adults, we learn we are split
many, many times, the way the seemingly solid
earth is cobbled
from massive plates gristly & moaning
at the faults. Our skulls only gradually
join, fissures fuse
to a solid dome of protective bone.

———•———

In French, earthquake is *tremblement*
de terre. Our "terror" comes
from the Greek, to tremble.
Those terrors that shake us
from sleep are the worst. We were so safe,
slept like Medea's children. Innocent
in dreams, we wake to her betrayal,
her truth: we are only fragile bones.

After hours, years, we rise
from the catacombs, free,
blink noonday sun like newborns,
cling to each other, touch
the simple joy of muscle
& flesh & heat of skin laid sweet
over these armatures of bone.

I love you more then
than I have ever loved
& know too, I must soon forget
or go mad.

OUR LADY OF THE PIGEONS

For DSJ

At the Piazza San Marco a woman stands,
arms horizontal, waiting
to take flight. Her hands are full of stale bread,
her body is suet. She can barely be seen
for the pigeons that cover her,
croon throaty promises,
rustle wings like wedding silk.
In her feather cocoon she wishes
her eyes were millet, offers them,
eager beaks peck,
swallow the gelatin of sight. Red feet clutch,
claws hold tight & all take flight at once
she ascends in a flurry of beating wings
the cathedral below her, jealous, landlocked stone.

BECOMING DAVID

for Michelangelo

In the Accademia's narrow gallery
men are born from stone, rough-hewn,
half-alive, strain to break free of

white rose marble. Pale skin taut
over bas-relief backbones, hands,
arms, crowns emerging, scapula

like nascent wings. Birth is hard
from rocks, they are deaf
to our cries, cold to our touch,

inert in the face of our struggle.

At the end of the great hall,
under the vaulted rotunda,
a sleek-muscled shepherd stands—

peak of our aspiration—
fully formed, rib cage inhaling
greatness, he has transmuted stone

into victory. Eyes burning, poised
colossal grace, weight easy
on forward foot, the young man expects

to be called king.

THE ASCENSION

In the azure above Siena, one thousand
sickle-winged swallows slant, swoop,
madly gorge on unseen insects—
open-mouthed ecstatics trill a
bel canto: "*bene, bene, bene,*"
food is on the wing, Sunday bells
from a dozen churches proclaim
God is just.

Pigeons, who rule the sky
in lesser towns like Venice,
lie low here, squat yellow-eyed
& seething on arch-tiled
terra cotta roofs & in niches
in faded brick walls. They coo,
bass-voiced in awkward envy,
cede the skies to the psalm-singing
masters of angle & slice.
The swallows rise, higher & higher,
become the ash of spent incense,
tiny black specks surrender
to a vaulted, cloudless sky.

With the Frogs at the Kladeos River in Ancient Olympia

The frogs are masters of disguise
at Kladeos—brown, dappled riverbank
until your shadow passes over, then
plop! they are one with rippling algae,
green silk like goddess hair, hidden
in crystal stream.

Look close & perhaps one will deign
to appear, chiseled head like fine green
Greek marble, bulbous eyes moist
black opals rimmed in gold eyelids.

Silent, he waits for the thousand eyes
of a blue dragonfly to mistake him
for a rock.

If you sit like them long enough,
quiet, muscled haunches thick
with grace, they may reward you
with a song. Not the craven croak
of fable or the jackdaw caw
of the harlequin hooded crows
in the eucalyptus overhead.

No, they will sing in chorused voices high
& lyre sweet of amphibian dreams,
of moving in two worlds at once,
of the musky poetry of flies—
sonnets in the whir of
insect wings.

They will sing the story of each stone
in the riverbed, its birth name, & the
smooth, polished name
it hides. They will speak
tadpole & ancient frog tongues
uncurl stories so serpentine that past
& present will eat each other's tails.

They will weave for you, with exquisite
hands on tiny forearms, green tapestries—
lime & algae, forest & grass, & water
will speak in these stories,
caress you, become you, breathe you
& you water, the sweet honey current
each ripple you & you will fill
& join the song & burst & fill again
& the sweet smooth chorus
from your throat will surprise you
& make you joy.

When you return to your world,
as you must, you will carry this song
in you, at carotid & temples,
tympani, stirrup & anvil—
to sing in the times when silence
will not suffice
& the fiction of a single world
is not enough.

LI PO & THE YELLOW RIVER

Li Po, they say, was a common drunk
who died embracing the dancing moon
reflected in the Yellow River.

Enchanted, lunatic, besotted on plum wine
& illusion, the old poet stripped
& leapt, arms wide, on that ravishing orb

as if on the woman from Ch'ang-an
who, he wrote: "has eyes more beautiful
than the moon, bare feet white as frost without

the stockings of the upper crust."[†] The moon
shattered & reformed, seemed woven,
then a wave, then flecks of sparkling jade—

trickster moon. All the water that ever was
still exists, in clouds, rain, ice,
in honeycomb caverns

beneath our pilgrim feet.
If I am lucky, the water that
embraced Li Po will find my lips.

[†] Translation by Sam Hamill © 1993

Friday the Laundress Said

she would no longer wash my
favorite shirt, the khaki cotton
with the pocket flaps, epaulets
& button tabs that
gathered the rolled-up sleeves.

"I cannot take responsibility,"
she said, Middle European
honor at stake. Her fingers probed
the sou-sized holes at the corners
of the pockets. She clucked at the
collar, not just frayed, but after
ten years, separated altogether.
& when she held the back in
front of her face, like Salome's veil,
the cloth revealed Salome's mustache
& crooked yellow teeth.

"This is cheap shirt," she eulogized,
"you can get another." "The Louvre,"
I said. "Pompeii. Michelangelo's *David*;
St. Peter's Square; Versailles buried
in autumn leaves. Four-in-the-morning
lightning across the face of a
Barcelona cathedral. A riot of pink
& purple cosmos in Monet's garden.
A loneliness so profound on a dock
in Salerno I thought I would die.
Lunch on a sun-bright terrace
in Mediterranean Spain with two
crazy film directors & twenty-two
kinds of mussels fresh from the sea.
A week in Sylvie's Paris bed, her yogi's
body bent in *asanas* of love, my
novice's bones barely able to keep
up, but my flesh was singing &
I had to follow."

The thin khaki cotton threads
pulsed under her fingers.

A slow nod, & she threw the
shirt on the scrap table, smiling,
satisfied. I left, to weave it
back together.

Sisyphus' Day Runner

SILENCE

Sometimes we forget the blessing of silence.
Sometimes the wind is poem enough,
the way a mountain hunches, the play
of sun across ocean in the space of a day.
Sometimes moss is a stanza, the orange of lichen
will stand in for a sestina on a day like that.

Sisyphus' Day Runner

Each morning gathers its own shape,
shoulders its own day despite my well-hewn
intention. "But it's all in this book," I argue,

"meticulously planned, careful
cursive on white-lined pages,
three-hole punched, bound into ox-blood

stained leather. Here is where
I should be. This hour is a sacred
precinct, a *temenos;* this hour is for

Mammon." But the pages don't care
what the ink commands. They remember
being trees, how sustenance comes

unbidden, the rhizomes, taproot,
capillary force the earth delivers when
needed. The leaves delight

in reminder paper cuts, sharp signals of who
is in charge. "After this many years, this many
thin lines," they whisper, amused,

"you'd think he would have learned."

PANTOUM FROM THE WOMAN IN WARD 13

I am advised by ravens who know
the questions before I can pose them;
flies are faster this year, elude my grasp
with an oblique ease previously unpossessed.

The questions before I can pose them
fragment, shatter & misbehave, dart off
with an oblique ease. Previously unpossessed
objects are inhabited by spirits of the dead.

Fragment, shatter & misbehave, dart off—
see if I care that illusion winks when
objects are inhabited by spirits of the dead,
when religion is suspect & my saving grace is to

see if I care that illusion winks when
truth hides behind my back. I need a good mirror
when religion is suspect & my saving grace is too
fragile, like butterfly wings beating against glass.

Truth hides behind my back. I need a good mirror
in this place, though doctors worry about edges,
fragile, like butterfly wings beating against glass
until their fine dust is spent & they are transparent.

In this place, though doctors worry about edges,
I still have a few tricks up my sleeve, I can live
until their fine dust is spent & they are transparent.
It's already happening. The last doctor they sent knew

I still have a few tricks up my sleeve. I can live
with watching them shimmer, blink out—
it's already happening. The last doctor they sent knew;
couldn't save herself for all her science & her breeding

flies are faster this year, elude my grasp.
I am advised by ravens who know.

All the Hits, All the Time

My brother fears the jukebox in his head,
cranking out perpetual Fifties hits,
the echoes of performers long since dead.

"I think I'm going nuts," he gravely said,
"from Frankie Lymon, all those Coasters bits."
My brother fears the jukebox in his head

is crowding out the brain cells that instead
should be applied to living by his wits,
not echoes of performers long since dead.

In his strained voice I hear that growing dread
of Jackie Wilson's apoplectic fits-—
my brother fears the jukebox in his head.

I joked that he should line his skull with lead,
block Frankie, Ricky, all those other twits—
those echoes of performers long since dead.

I'll never cop that I'm forever fed
by Sixties flashbacks, Cream & acid hits.
I dearly love the jukebox in *my* head,
it flies the Airplane & the Grateful Dead.

THE PSYCHIATRIST, NARCISSUS, WRITES UP HIS FINDINGS ON JEKYLL & HYDE

It wasn't Mr. Hyde's fault, despite
the biographer's slant. It was
Jekyll. Addicted, he was, to the taste
of remorse. He loved his dram
each morning, ruing his evening's
conduct, but nonetheless feeling
superior to the man he'd become
the night before. We all must feel
superior to someone, why not
ourselves? Why not ourselves
at the center of the universe? Our victims
certainly feel less than *we* do. Besides, it is we
who have fallen from grace, deserving
pity for our broken wings.

One of a Chorus of Angels

I am the angel of doubt
whose slow resurrection
is an everyday miracle.

My wings, appearing clipped
each evening, are majestic
again by dawn; opaque they

block the sun. Feel them spread
around you, mimicking comfort,
familiar as the low murmuring

of mother, as father's hard-won
homilies. I teach your true
potential, urge you to reach

no farther than you really can.
This is a hard life, disappointment
the fate of most; there is not

enough to go around. Keep your head
low against my incorruptible breast,
seek solace in my encircling wings.

I am protection, sweet child, a feather
bed for you to sleep away
the trying, excruciating pain.

CHILDHOOD SUNDAY SERMONS

Dick Tracy, square-beaked beacon
of justice, crimestopper
in a lurid world
of misshaped miscreants,
fists & bullets his tools in
a simpler pre-Miranda universe.

Dagwood boasted clean suburban lines,
well-stocked fridge, perpetual nap—
hate your boss & your work. The happy
klutz needed saving—or scolding—
from his well-coifed wife. Neighborly
fist fights over power tools—poker to make up.

Prince Valiant, pageboyed knight of the
swift sword, brooded in dark & somber
blues & violets. Despite home & queen
he wandered a chiaroscuro world,
doing good—yet still gravid
with lonely power.

Krazy Kat was felled by bricks of love,
as we all would be one day. We didn't know
as children how much courage it would take
to succumb to the love of mice, if we were
cats—or for we mice to lose ourselves
in that sweet, carnivorous, feline breath.

THOUGHTS WHILE UNPACKING
AFTER SEPTUM UNDEVIATION

Mother had good reason to advise
against sticking beans up your nose.
You could lose the whole farm
there, not just beans, but corn,
broccoli, parsnips, a year's crop. Sinuses have
more square footage than the average
New York City walkup. Prime territory
to lose eyeglasses, suitcases, whole tribes
wandering still—the first Virginia
colony—every unmatched sock
since the 19th Century
invention of washing machines. Astonished
astronomers report outer space is more
dark matter than visible stuff, an analogy
up to snuff as it relates to that iceberg tip
in mid-face. Mother was right, any child
who would act like you has
holes in their head—you just never knew
how big.

The Proctor Will Have Instructions

There is a test
at the end of this
life. Don't worry, it's impossible
to fail. They'll ask
what you learned & we all
learned something. It will be
multiple choice,
you'll have a quiet room,
a sharp black number two
pencil & all
the time you need.

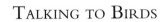

TALKING TO BIRDS

BIRDWATCHING WITH MARLEY

I am a more avid birder
than my cat. You wouldn't know it
at first, watching me reclined in my wicker

rocker, him on his strong haunches, orange
ears alert, us side-by-side on the second-story
porch, ogling into the nearby Bishop pine at the

two-toned Black Phoebe, with its sharp bill,
dark cowl & shocking white chest.
Or admiring the ubiquitous black-bibbed

House Sparrow with black mask & symmetrical
chestnut patches like decoration on a gladiator's
helmet. I see appreciation in Marley's

sapphire eyes, the way they narrow
with pleasure, as mine do, when a
Mourning Dove ventures close to offer

its whispery, sighing song. He loves the songs
so much he will sometimes keep a vigil
at the base of the porch wall, outside

the bird's line of sight, white fur
attentive, muscled body quivering
like a violin string, concealed, like Cyrano,

from all but the lovely voice of Roxanne.
There are even times when he's moved
to dance, boogie back & forth on his

hind legs, beating a tattoo of unfettered
joy at his communion with the Rosy Finch
a mere six feet away among

the waxy magnolia leaves.
Sometimes, he'll even leap
to the porch rail, smile with all his

teeth, & pace north, then south, tail flicking
in time to the mad glissandos
of a Mockingbird. But then—

& this surprises me—
he will suddenly turn tail, as if sated, & leave
me to bask alone, warm in my own

patch of sunlight, imagining myself a cat,
but apparently more patient. I'll often see
him later, sulking downstairs under the rosebush,

as if doing penance, punishing himself
with thorns for his understandable
ecstasy, his longing eyes almost always

turned toward heaven.

Ordinary Birds

They are constant & we forget
just how steady. They answer dawn
with diapason, carry trees place to place

in unsuspecting bellies,
teach distance & the miracle
of return. Silence is illusion,

grace notes always ring somewhere,
gold amidst bronze & steel gray,
crimson counterpoint to a chlorophyll

world, white clarion cries sharp
against undulant ocean blue. Raphael painted
St. Michael rampant, spear raised,

feet steady on a demon's back, balanced
by triumphant feathered wings of blue
& gold & orange—like a glorious tropical bird.

What did Raphael *know*?

ON GUARDIAN ANGELS

Perhaps my angels have all along been birds.
How often am I out of their sight?
Even when I'm indoors, they come
to the window, seek me, keep watch.

So what if I can't understand their speech?
As long as the dawn hears the rooster & the waves
take their cue from the gulls, I too can have
their music without demanding sense of it.

In the main, my angels are small, brown sparrows,
who fly like tiny grapeshot & fastidiously watch,
but call little attention to themselves. They even seem
indifferent; but isn't that a perfect disguise?

TALKING TO BIRDS

Newscaster said last night
a woman in Arizona was teaching
birds to talk. Really talk, she says,
not mimic human speech.

I would prefer to speak the language
of birds, than to have them know mine.
Listen as eagles express exhilaration
at hovering for hours on thermal currents.
How many words they have for "soar."

Speak to sparrows about nesting,
intricate interlacing
of string & twig,
the warmth of the young,
their incessant mouths.

Hear geese describe the holy longing
we call migration, how it starts in the soul
spreads through thorax to wingtips
until flight is only a matter of rising
& following. Hear owls recount the crunch
of tiny bones, the joy of slicing talon
through fur striking
in soft silence, feeling the final
shudder before the food
relaxes into surrender.

Hear roseate flamingos relate,
so matter-of-fact,
the miracle of turning & weaving
by the thousands
in flocks so large
they sunder earth from sun, yet
they never touch in flight.

I suspect birds have different dialects,
but that their words for war
& love may surprise us
in their similarity.

GREAT-GRANDMOTHER IN HER SUNDAY PLUMED HAT

In the time before Starlings spread
their iridescent shadow across the homes
of Eastern Bluebirds & Great Crested
Flycatchers, & the Passenger
Pigeon still flew, great-grandmother rolled
her head from side to side, cried out, sweating,
knees high, water broken, & pushed grandfather
into this abundant world. Birds covered the
sky like a comforter. Ladies then did not
lust, but they coveted magnificent
plumes from Great & Snowy Egrets
& adorned their hats with feathers of terns
& grebes, White Pelicans & Albatross. In this
picture, circa 1905, great-grandmother's head
is an avian adventure while grandfather itches
in short wool pants. Her face itself, bone white
& sharp-edged as English china, has an egret's
profile, a steady, measured, hunter's gaze allowing
nothing to escape.

THE QUAIL

I'm sorry if this is vague,
but I was young. The old woman had
white hair, curled tight to her head like a
bathing cap. Her house was dark,
wood. My mother befriended her
through church, ran errands, brought
casseroles, stood by as she lost
one leg & then
the other. When she was near death,
her son, whom no one had known
about, showed up, wondered loud
about his mother's sparse house,
why the deed was in my mother's name.
But that is not the story.

I want to tell how the old woman,
made tinier by the surgeries,
propped in bed against white lace
pillows, smiled at me, pursed
her lips, made her mouth small &
whistled *Chi-ca-go* in three
soft syllables to let me
know what the quail in the trees
outside her room were crying.

Requiem: Cypress Point, Carmel

In this depression formed by two sandstone
boulders, gold & gray, we each cup a handful

of ash & rose petals from a hammered
copper box, arc them into the green-glazed

sea where kelp sways like hair brushing a young
girl's shoulder. Waves crash & echo, mask her

father's voice, save for the keening. When he
turns back to land it is pitched low again.

He reminds her friends of all they have to
live for, begs them not to follow her lead.

The tide pushes in & in, & we help each other
clamber up the rocks to safe ground.

A heron stands out on the water, rides swells
on a piece of driftwood we can't see.

We watch the ocean as though she is going
to come back.

THE ARTIST'S WAY

*"Composition is the art of arranging, in a decorative manner,
the various elements at the artist's disposal."*
                                        —Henri Matisse

In Cartier-Bresson's photograph of Matisse
my eye goes first to the doves.
Slightly unfocused,
stippled white, three dominate
the upper right
of this decisive frame.

They perch on the round
top of a tubular wire cage.
Their crown & wing feathers
sport tufts, as a breeze ruffles in
from the sliver of window behind;
or they molt for the camera,
shed feathers in a flutter of release.

Two doves watch Bresson
sidelong, necks cocked in cautious grace.
The third shows a perfect three-quarter face:
imperious, the white queen poses.

My gaze drifts left, & then
beyond the half of frame the birds own,
I pass into the painter's space:
The white-whiskered old man,
in a heavy cloth coat, knit scarf,
white-banded wool cap, sits in an unseen chair.
Above him, another cage, this one square,
with a smudge of light. Perhaps
a fourth dove? Behind him, to his right,
another cage, pagoda-topped,
this one bent cane, & empty.

Surrounded by cages, Matisse studies
a fifth dove, held in his left hand
like a flute of champagne, its image
mirrored in each lens
of his rimless glasses.

His right forefinger
& thumb the shape of a teardrop,
he touches pen to a page
in the huge sketchbook on his lap.
His dove, wings hunched
like a shoulder shrug, is one
black eyespot, expressionless
in an asymmetric field of white,
still for the old man's
scrutiny: a wild beast held
in his focused, loving grip.

It is 1944,
& the world needs doves
now more than ever.

MENTAL BLOCK

" . . . and whatsoever Adam called
every living creature, that was
the name thereof."
Genesis 2:19 KJV

I forgot the names of birds
from fortnight to fortnight,
& had to look again

at well-thumbed field guides—
remind myself, chide myself
for faulty memory. Until they

spoke: *We are not "birds,"*
they said, *We are*
astonishment, delight,

distant cousins at your reunion—
familiar, but your given name
takes wing from our minds, too.

Summer Rain Sonnet for the Average Housefly

"The housefly (Musca domestica) can complete its life cycle in as little as seven to ten days."

—Newspaper Filler Item

When it rains, thick gobbets that plunk
on the sill with the cadence of childhood
jump rope rhymes, even flies stay home.
And where is that, exactly? Small fecal castles?
A welcoming calf's carcass, smooth ribs brown
& regular as a bone marimba,
enough leather clinging to struts
for a makeshift umbrella? No. Let's say
home is the heaped white sweetness
of a giant sugar bowl, each crystal a cubist
delight a thousand times sweeter
in compound eyes—each short *Musca domestica* life,
though confined a day by rainfall, not brutish
at all, but tasty & worth a song of its own.

REFLECTIONS ON A DECEMBER SUNDAY

Even the wind is uncertain, flutters
andante in the neighbor's chimes, then backs
off to the cirrus-streaked coast, ponders its
next move, like the cat with all the time
in the world worrying that dying
fly down at the baseboard where sloughed skin cells
& hair clot together, accumulating
enough evidence to accuse you
of neglect.

        South, in the middle distance,
airplanes strain just a little bit harder,
shiver in the intermittent headwind;
wings quiver, takeoff angle just a
little more acute, passengers' palms a
touch sweatier, riveted skins groan
as the flaps push down & the wheels nestle up.

When the wind shifts & picks up sage
from the east, the chimes play dead, like that fly,
& the temperature jumps ten degrees.
The sky is pale blue again
& cumulus blow out of the humbled path
the sun makes through winter. The cat bats once,
twice, stuns the fly, then feigns indifference,
like the wind, like the passenger in seat
20A who sees my house from fifteen
hundred feet as just another golden
window in a net of jewels. He even thinks
"net of jewels," then his mind scurries back to
"safety net" as the plane banks right, his
stomach lurches, & more windows explode.

The fly is large & green,
lumbering toward the end of his seven-day
life, measured now, it appears, in the distance
between one white paw & the other.
The cat decides it's endgame, opens black
irises abysmally wide, pink tonguetip
visible through slightly parted teeth. Presto,
the chimes erupt, the wind is back, the cat
is startled, & the fly, sudden despite
decrepitude, rises like a Sikorsky,
eludes the cat's balletic leap, vectors
out the louvered window, shivering slightly
in the headwind, alive & heading
sunward, its thousand-faceted eye
reflecting glory.

AUBADE

In your leopard-skin silk pajamas
(with the scarlet piping at the sleeves
& lapels), you waved goodbye

from our balcony at dawn—
a sudden, extravagant gesture, regal,
both arms high, love triumphant,

& released from the sidewalk magnolia
a scattering of doves neither of us
knew was there. They fluttered, jubilant,

whistling at the light from your face,
which they took
to be the sun.

LIEBESTOD

I Burn for You

I know why people spontaneously
combust. Their amalgamate of flesh
& gas no match
for the heat of the ecstatic.
We each remember
the Big Bang, ache to recapitulate
that primeval first time. Every synapse ignites—
chain reaction—the dark meat
bursts with enlightenment.

There will be no Rapture;
just a timeless torch song.

OPOSSUM

for KK

A black & white Dalmatian-
spotted opossum, sharp at
nose & long pink tail,
meanders, barrel-bodied,
across our quiet street, skirts
edge of the neighbor's lawn,
disappears, king of nonchalance,
past impatiens & agave plant,
around the corner of the brick
foundation.

My love is an opossum, unexpected,
oddly shaped, close to the ground
& somehow resolute, certain of itself,
& you.

SHE ASKS US BOTH TO IMAGINE THE RELATIONSHIP WON'T LAST

None of this ever happened.
The man & woman never met,
juices never mingled
hearts never beat together.
In the beginning,
world never started turning,
darkness stayed without form
& void. God missed
his cue. Infinite number of
monkeys never got born, no
typewriters got invented, Shakespeare
didn't get written. Blake, Whitman
never sang. Your eyes were never
blue.

In India the Stone Temple Gods

act much like people
in love. They enfold each other
in postures of grace, unashamed
yoni & lingam,
round at breast & thigh, couple
after couple in emulation of stork
& snake & jasmine vine. Their eyebrows arched
like their supple
spines, nostrils full
of the scent of the beloved,
lips full can speak
no other words but the murmur
of corpuscle & membrane
flushed with bliss. Their biscuit skin
rouged at cheek & forehead, their eyes
evolved beyond pupil & iris, reflect
the secret seen at the moment
of remembering
why we were all arranged
in this immortal frieze.

Come, my wife, teach me again how to act
as gods, turn to golden stone
& bliss.

LIEBESTOD

I.

It's just greed, I know. I want it all,
forever. I want the wonder
of the hummingbird clicking & whistling
each morning at the feeder—
speed & thrumming music
of its wings, the tiny drop of sweet nectar
on its needle beak as it hovers,
raises its head,
feels the delicious trickle
in its silver & purple throat that scatters
sunrise—light
from a ballroom globe. I want forever
the sparrow's dance
among the magnolia's waxed green
& leather orange leaves,
effortless hop from branch to branch,
side-to-side head dips as it rubs its conical beak
on a rough patch of bark. I want my lips
to brush the pulse in the hollow
of your throat, your fingers warm
on my skin, my heart expanding
under your gaze.

II.

There is a face
in the magnolia this morning
that is, really,
only shadows on the bottom
of a wrinkled orange leaf
in the flat October sunrise. Its right eye,
just a hollow;
its nose the leaf's central ridge;
its surprised, slightly open mouth
—asking the gods for more time—
is a small imperfection,
the leaf beginning to curl in on itself,
lips visible only now. It is that face
some see on the desert planet Mars—
a trick of light on rock weathered
by solar wind. It is my face,
lit for a brief moment.

ABOUT THE AUTHOR

Richard Beban turned to poetry in 1993 after more than thirty years as a journalist, then a television and screen writer. He holds a BA in Liberal Studies, and an MFA in Creative Writing from Antioch University, Los Angeles.

His poetry has appeared since 1994 in more than forty-five periodicals and literary Websites, and in sixteen national anthologies, and he has been nominated for a Pushcart Prize.

With his wife, the writer Kaaren Kitchell, and three other poets, he helped organize and run one of Los Angeles' most successful weekly reading series at Venice's Rose Cafe, and he and Kitchell produced the 2003 Freshwater Marsh Ecopoetry Celebration at Playa Vista, California in a five-hour celebration of the new freshwater marsh constructed to help restore Ballona Wetlands.

He has been a featured reader at more than fifty venues, from the Los Angeles County Museum of Art, to Berkeley's Cody's Books, to Shakespeare & Company, Paris.

He and Kitchell, who co-authored a non-fiction book on mythology, run a monthly poetry and fiction workshop series in their living room in Playa del Rey, California.